Introduction - Location

The Double Trouble philosophy throughout many of our booklets has been to propose isolating and focussing on particular themes to enable a number of ideas to be absorbed and developed. This equally applies to the subject of 'locations'. Such an approach helps a deeper understanding, along with integrity, to limit the chance to flit from one subject to another in a superficial way. It can also give a creator time to work on several approaches, allowing space to engage the subject and not feel that everything but the kitchen sink' needs to be included in one piece of work.

Over the years, subjects have been suggested to college classes and to our readers within this series of books. These have proved helpful, encouraging the recipients to actually start a sketchbook by not being so overwhelmed. It is so easy for people to feel stifled and intimidated by being expected to draw in the first instance a view of extensive landscapes, the perspective challenges of buildings or the relationship of shapes between groups of figures. It is no wonder so many are put off from drawing forever. It is always best to start simply and aim to 'walk' before you can 'run'. As you may have noted previously, some titles such as 'Trees as a Theme', 'Red', 'Colour Explorations' and 'New Dimensions' and many of the others too, contain this constant plea. Other helpful sketchbook themes suggested by our friend and colleague, Louise Baldwin have included 'Spots and Stripes', 'Borders and Edges' and 'Networks and Meshes'. The information collected was most inspiring. Taking the mystique away allowed some fabulous colours, patterns and textures to

be taken out of context providing really useful references for a range of future projects. It is amazing how mini themes such as these can provoke a total re-look at familiar surroundings and help to build up both skills, confidence and more importantly true enjoyment and sense of achievement. Whether at home or somewhere exotic, it is hoped that being more aware of your location and taking advantage of some unexpected features will enrich your visual vocabulary.

There are times when we need to sketch away from home. These occasions can be planned or unplanned but by carrying a small sketchbook at all times a significant thought or image need not go unrecorded. If there is no sketchbook handy then any scrap of paper, old envelope etc. can be used. Improvisation can lead to a more relaxed style of drawing as the materials are not so precious.

A little preparation beforehand will mean that the visual notes or sketchbook/diary will be more effective. The type of paper, size and format of the book may influence the way of working and there are many options. A new format or different drawing media could stimulate a fresh approach. At times there will only be moments for fleeting glimpses whilst at others there may be an opportunity for prolonged observation. In this book there are examples of unusual materials and spontaneous responses to situations. Sometimes the results have more energy because they are outside the tried and tested methods. It is helpful to remain open to the new possibilities another location might offer. At times painting and preparing

pages in advance might enrich the experience. This involves painting a colour wash on the paper reflecting the background of the subject to be recorded. (see sketchbooks on page 22)

If there are historical aspects, researching the background beforehand may mean that it is possible to tap into the atmosphere of the place most effectively.
The important thing is the focussed looking and some way of recording it so that it will be useful for future reference. You can exaggerate features that excite you and refer to photographs for colour and context but it is those immediate reactions that record your unique viewpoint and experience and will probably be the most meaningful for future work.

Top: This sketch of looking through trees was made initially with a pencil, pen and accompanying notes. The colour and texture gels were applied later to replicate the lichen having exaggerated the scale and pattern in situ.

Above: The close ups of two types of tree bark were interpreted by gluing layers of textured papers, which were coloured with Koh-i-Noor and crayons. Acrylic wax was applied on some areas.

Setting out

Mapping the route

Every aspect of a trip can offer the possibility for inspiration. Keeping a travel journal, either literary or visual, may become a pleasurable habit for many people. It records and enhances a journey and relieves the potential tedium of travel.

Notes and quick sketches can record aspects of interest, which can be further developed when there is time.
Photographs may help to reinforce impressions but are rarely as personal as immediate responses.

Digital photography has meant that instant references can be made when required. It is good to work in situ and such photographs are helpful when used to confirm images at a later stage.

Often the mapping of the journey is a good introduction to the context of the location. Colours and foliage may change along with land formations and rock structures, particularly on a long journey. Just recording the principal colours in simple blocks can be a most effective record of a passing landscape (see 4, far right).

Maps hold great fascination for many and topographical references can have iconic status and be useful when establishing a sense of place.

Air travel can be relentless but on long haul trips where there is daylight it is marvellous to have a window seat from which to observe the world from above. On various flights across India, USA, Australia and New Zealand the patterns and colours have been breathtaking and a source of great inspiration.

Having the appropriate materials to record this information needs careful advance planning and a fine line pen and aquarelle pencils are always useful. With a brush and water the images may be further enhanced.

Improvising

Travel, particularly by air, often necessitates a radical pruning of art materials but in transit it is possible to collect a range of items that could prove useful. Airports always contain pens, pencils, notebooks, glues and magazines that could later be used for collage.

Seat pockets on aircraft also have magazines with good basic maps and even an 'emergency bag' that could be used if pressed as a source of art material.

Plastic knives and the free toothbrushes are excellent as glue spreaders and for applying textural surfaces.
Hotels often have small marmalade and jam pots that serve as water pots and the plastic (no longer needed) hotel keys make wonderful printed and dragged marks. There are usually notepads and paper and a courtesy sewing kit that could also prove useful.

These items combined with twigs, feathers, paper bags and other locally found materials offer the possibility of a huge variety of mark making tools and surfaces.

It might prove interesting to make a visual diary using only found materials and allow for spontaneous responses to a new environment that could result in fresh and rewarding imagery.

1) Written and visual notes of a coach journey, in Tunisia, to the Sahara desert. Water colour on water colour paper with pencil and fine line pen.

2) An assemblage of improvised drawing media including a collage made from local maps, brown paper bags, hotel notepads, used plastic room key, marmalade pot, aircraft toothbrush, plastic knife, twigs, makeup sponges and airport chopsticks for improvised knitting needles.

3) A cloth comprised of buttonhole rings worked over fingers and joined together by knotting and wrapping. This was worked on a long coach journey and echoed some of the rhythms of the organic forms of the changing landscape.

4 A local free map served as a background for this colour strip reflecting the change of colours on a prolonged coach journey from Ballarat to Mildura in Australia.

(4)

(1)

Learning to look

Sometimes students expect to be struck by a thunderbolt creating a vision to draw. We continually suggest that really learning to observe is the starting point. Initially this sounds humdrum but it can be very effective. Harnessing passion and discipline in order to focus your looking takes time and practice. Even those of us who have drawn for years need to apply these very same rules if sketching has been side stepped for a while due to other commitments. It can be hard and frustrating as it takes time to attain the same standards as previously.

Wherever you can pause for a while, allow yourself to really look around and unexpected sources of design, a spectacular colour scheme or a surprising image will immerge. Whether you are waiting in a queue, sitting in your garden or away on holiday, try and take time to organise your observations.

With so many thoughts to consider, the following headings can be helpful by limiting the many confusing scenes that may be before you.

LOOKING UP
LOOKING AHEAD
LOOKING TO THE RIGHT AND THEN THE LEFT
LOOKING DOWN
LOOKING THROUGH
LOOKING CLOSELY

Zoom in as with a close up lens so restricting too wide a view and selecting fewer aspects to consider.

To illustrate this point, a small chapel (seen above) on the Greek island of Lesbos, offering shade from the blistering sun, presented the chance to sketch every morning and late afternoon. Disciplined looking was applied. Over two weeks, almost all information, filling a sketchbook was gathered from one or other side of the chapel. Sitting on the nearside, looking back along the road past the harbour and towards the village was continually fascinating to observe but too much to take in to draw so the suggestions above were considered.

LOOKING TO THE RIGHT was a corn coloured hillside with many clumps of rounded shrubs, tufts of tawny grasses, interspersed with rocks and pebbles and short blond stubble. Due to the position of the early morning sun, these bright hues contrasted with the dark shapes of the shadows cast from a stone wall. This view was fascinating during the whole of the stay at this location, as colour and tonal elements changed with the time of day.

However, LOOKING DOWN and just ahead, an area of partially worn away cracked paving, a collection of chards and dried grasses strewn around appeared quite ordinary at first glance but was intriguing to record. On reflection later, the muted colours and networks could be developed into a variety of appealing patterns.

The far side of the chapel offered an array of opportunities. LOOKING AHEAD was a rock face that showed extraordinary, elegant etched markings that could be appreciated in the diffused morning shade whereas in the full afternoon sun it celebrated glorious ochre colours and strong rock structures, ridges and indentations.
Looking at the foreground, the rocks and rounded boulders stretched down to the sea. On walking over them and LOOKING DOWN, crevices harbouring a detritus of smaller rocks and stones showed interesting contrasting textures. The rust coloured markings offered an attractive alternative to the greys and tiny areas of unexpected pink.

Sketchbooks 1 & 3. Parts of the two rock sketches were built up with paper shapes that made it easier to suggest the dimensional surfaces. Koh-i-Noor and aquarelle crayons were used to colour the images and also the rock face seen right (2).

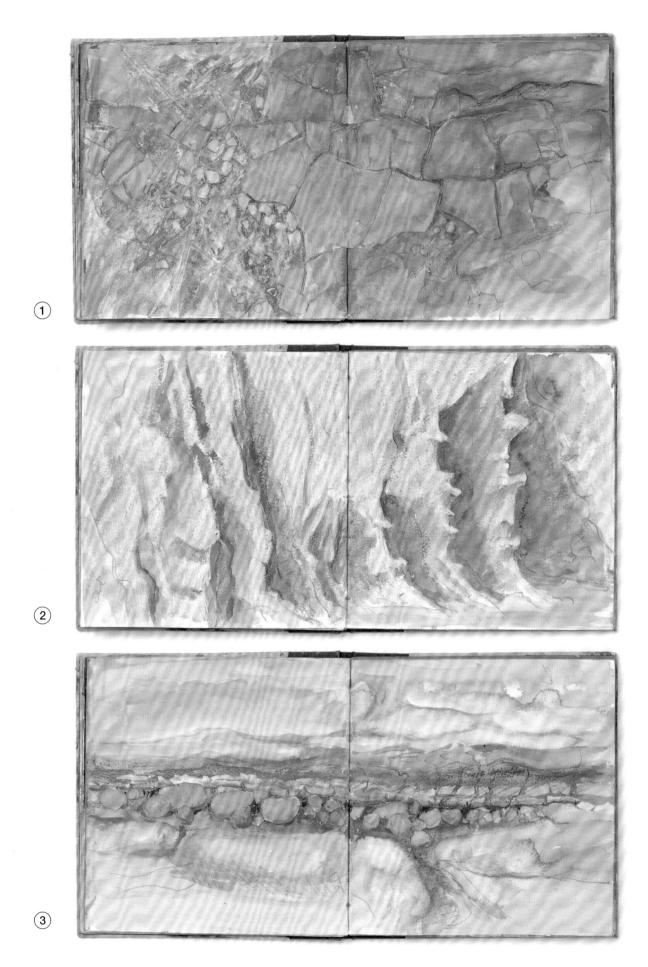

1

2

3

The other side of the chapel presented differing views.

LOOKING TO THE LEFT was another section of the hillside covered in rounded mounds of a particular shrub exploiting silvers, greys and ginger hues growing in and around a traditional stone wall.

LOOKING TO THE RIGHT was a clear view of a craggy headland and the sea. It is always totally absorbing trying to capture the ever-changing colours and textures of the water and could take a life's work. Making an interlude to watch this timeless beauty is therapeutic and uplifting. The subtle tones could easily revitalise your colour palette for so many projects.

Taking the term LOOKING DOWN literally on to the stone seat from where all these sketches started revealed a wonderful textural surface of plaster and paint. Grids, tiny eroded shapes, unexpected areas between them and brush strokes provided an amazing array of pattern. It was so surprising to realise that it had taken four to five days of sitting on this platform once or twice a day before noticing this unusual and exciting surface. This was evidence to support the notion that staying close within one location can be so beneficial. Allowing you to quietly get to know and feel a place helps to give real insight into the surroundings.

Both the hillside and sea sketches were created using pencil, aquarelle crayons and gouache. Silver gouache paint was used to capture the sparkle of the sea.

Pencils, torn paper shapes glued in place and paint was employed to create the intriguing surface of the ledge seat.

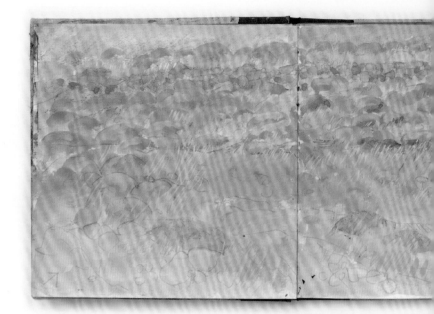

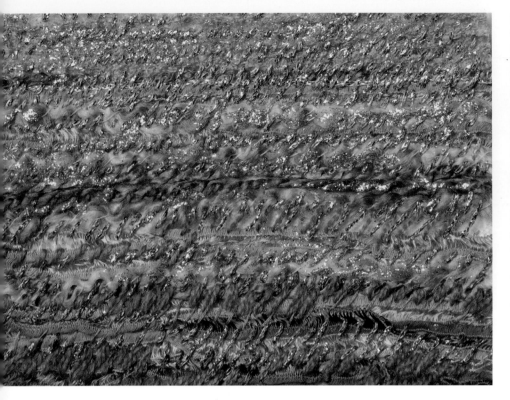

Off to Alaska

Receiving an invitation to teach on a cruise from Vancouver to Alaska was surprising, exciting and proved to be most enjoyable and a little bit challenging.
The only real time to sketch was early morning or evening when the ship was sailing to the next destination. During this particular trip, the weather was quiet and passive. Many lingering memories come to the fore. The seascapes were absolutely amazing. Words that come to mind include peaceful, serene, atmospheric and calm.

Due to being mainly on the move and not having enough time to actually draw, selecting to write brief notes and descriptive words as listed can be an extremely effective method of recording the surroundings.

'horizontal lines fractured by mountains and tree clad foothills breaking through the atmospheric ribbons of mist.'
'at times the sea, misty strips of land and the sky appear almost the same tone with just a subtle change of hue'.
'one evening, the water glowed all tones of gold'
'the sea was coloured all shades of grey, mid grey, dove, silvers through to steel blue'.
'closer to shore, the water appeared jade green sometimes with a blush of pink due to reflections of the rock and the mineral content'.
'the surface of the water was sometimes like glass interspersed with stripes of gentle flurries of ripples'.

First sketches, shown far right, were marked down quickly using a soft pencil with full notes on colour and texture. At a later time some were developed further within the confines of the cabin. On returning home the paintings, shown right, were developed just by relying on strong memories and descriptive notes so as not to over complicate the imagery with details.

Glacier Bay bathed in bright sunshine presented views in every direction and they were awesome. Although the glaciers with their amazing structures and unexpected turquoise colourings were spectacular, no actual detailed drawing was done as every minute needed to be savoured. Visual memories and a camera were used to capture the amazing imagery and atmosphere. On reaching home, the photographs and digital imagery were good but it was seeing them in conjunction with written notes and hurried sketches that really brought them back to life in a personal way.

Gouache paints and Koh-i-Noor were used to create the three sketches illustrated right.
The aim was to create simple atmospheric images.

The stitched sketch above was made by placing varying yarns horizontally onto the sticky surface of 'Aquabond' soluble material and topped with a transparent soluble film. Diagonal stitching was worked in a variety of threads to simulate the water patterns as well as joining all elements in order to create a fabric after the soluble materials are washed away. (see Book 17, Grids to Stitch) Glitter glue was used to highlight the sparkle of the water.

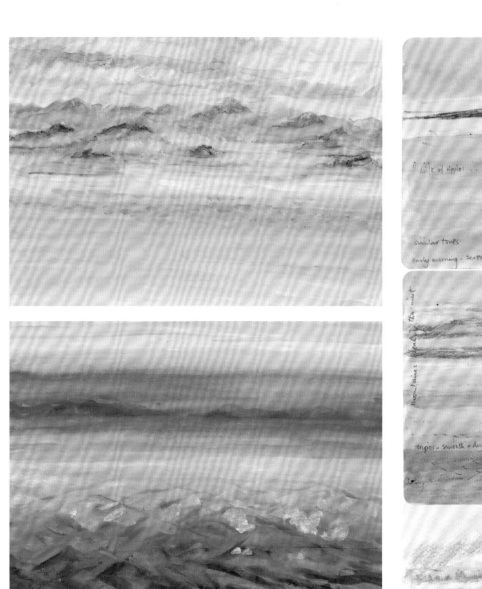

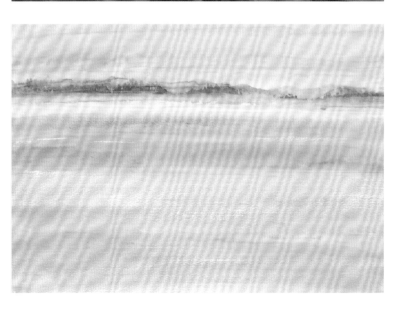

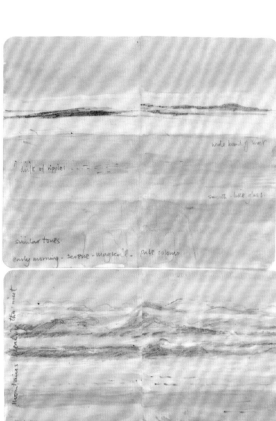

Postcards from

The postcard is a familiar and almost iconic item that immediately indicates travel. On holiday there is sometimes an element of obligation and guilt as friends and family may have expectations of some form of communication and the postcard has, in the past, been the obvious choice although in this technical age things may change.

It gives an impression of a place, a fleeting view and sometimes can be a cliché. However it is universally recognised and collections of postcards containing a bank of social history may be used to good effect in work that seeks to evoke travel, communication or even sentimentality.

Postcard size and format could be exploited as well as the stamps, postmarks, franking and airmail marks.
It is still possible to buy long concertinaed postcards that depict several views and more information.

Before travel, a simulated zigzag format of drawing paper could be used as a sketchbook that records the journey in a contained, compact way. This may be constructed from maps or travel pamphlets etc. and jesso or acrylic paint used as a wash to provide a drawing surface.

Water colour postcard blanks, available from most art shops, are excellent for water colour, mixed media and collage and could be used instead of a sketchbook. Standard, thinner postcard blanks are also useful.

When using the mixed media, consideration should be given to the type of background so that it may support the length and weight of the piece. Vilene, 'Lutradur' and some specialised papers can work well with this format. If less firm fabrics are to be used they may be supported with any of the previously mentioned materials for the final presentation.

Other aspects of a journey such as labels are also effective in conveying a sense of travel and location.

1) Postcard blank with coloured pencils describing wave formations and a hotel sewing kit used to add stitched marks.
The improvised use of luggage labels to make a travel diary.

2) A series of Australian impressions worked on watercolour postcard blanks and using 'Koh-i-Noor' dyes.

3) A set of Alaskan postcards on a ground of Lutradur. Bondaweb was painted with acrylic paint to simulate the dramatic sea, sky and landscape before being ironed onto the Lutradur.

The surfaces were then foiled with silver and stitched by hand and machine to complete. (See Book 3, Bonding and Beyond).

4) Zigzagged 'Postcard from a Vanishing Land'. Mixed media on a 'Lutradur' ground and a heat tool used to erode the surface.

Lake Mungo Retreat

On a recent trip to Australia we were offered the opportunity of participating in a group visit to Lake Mungo, an archaeological place of great importance. It is a World Heritage site situated in south western New South Wales. The lake, which stretches for miles, dried up around 16,000 years ago and there is evidence of human occupation from 36,000 years ago to the present day.

The lake basin is full of salt resistant plants mainly Black Blue Bush and is frequented by emus, kangaroo and many types of snake. The lake is partially edged on one side by a 'lunette' (crescent shaped) of magnificent sand and stone formations. The chance to study somewhere as exciting and beautiful as this was not to be missed.

The party, led by Glenys Mann, an Australian textile artist, comprised artists and teachers who relished the opportunity to work in such a remote and special environment. Liz Jeneid, another Australian artist with unique knowledge, was there to add an unobtrusive but perceptive input whenever required. Each member of the party had a different agenda but all wished to make the most of an exceptional experience.

Ancient peoples used the limited resources at their disposal with ingenuity and resourcefulness as their survival depended on it. The Aboriginal peoples are very proud of their heritage and take a major part in the management of this national park. Improvisation was key if we were to make the most of this visit.

Most members of the party kept a visual record and some had prepared books having researched the area beforehand. Others determined to use photography as their main means of recording images and impressions.

Our intention was to remain open to the sights and sensations and record them honestly in appropriate ways.

Among the group was a strong contingent who use natural dyes as a major dynamic of their work. This could have been a sensitive issue as we were in a national park and it was made very clear that we were to remove nothing, however small or apparently insignificant. They took the precaution of gaining permission beforehand to remove plant material from outside the park.

1) Glenys Mann supervising the dye pots over a barbecue.

2) Tied orange wool blanket prepared for the dye pot.

3) When steeped dried and untied the fabric formed natural folds that resembled the dune like formations and these were overcast to form more permanent rhythms.

4) Sketchbook pages from the very battered Mungo sketchbook.

It was fascinating to watch them improvise dye pots in a barbeque trough. Those who travelled by car brought old iron and aluminium pots and others found a local recycling area that had containers they could use. They used no toxic mordants to fix the natural vegetation and mallee bark, relying instead on steeping the fabrics and fibres for lengthy periods of time. The colour varied depending on whether an iron or aluminium pot was used. The resulting colours were subtle and organic and reflected the environment thus inspiring a whole range of textile treatments.

Jean's approach

The dramatic landscape and relentless climate showed the power of sun and water to forge fissures and features and it was appropriate to use methods of recording and mark making that reflected this.

The paint was poured and dripped onto the pages and marks made with sticks in order to achieve a degree of rawness. Tearing and cutting also seemed to reflect the erosion and layering of the sandy surfaces in an immediate way. A small bound notebook was selected for its size and weight and turned out to be unsuitable as the pages came out with the rough treatment but somehow it seemed fitting to the drama of the place. The most memorable moments were spent when Jan and I walked to the edge of the dried up lake bed to watch the sun rise over the lunette. The early light threw long shadows over exotic formations and we were the only people as far as the eye could see in a serene and silent world. The notebook was just a means of responding and recording, not an end in its own right but the effort of careful looking and reflecting gave a much more honest impression than numerous photographs and later really helped to recall the sights and impressions of a truly special experience.

④

Jan's Approach

Lake Mungo is one of the most enticing places seen so far and we both felt the special magic of the area.

Over time the actions of water, wind and ice have moved the sand and mud creating staggeringly impressive pinnacles. These ridged and creviced structures suggest dimensional stitching or pleated and tucked fabrics to mimic the patterns and textures. Sinewy rock and sand formations of many variations surround the site. The colours in daylight are a range of creams, greys, pinks and ochres which appear in rich warm hues at sunrise and sunset leaving lingering memories of reds, oranges as well as the ochres. Strong features that appealed were the amazing colours of the long shadows made by the sand turrets, shrubs and other vegetation at dawn and dusk. They appeared green, grey and in fleeting moments of exceptional light almost emerald green and turquoise. These combinations of complementary colours continually fascinate.

Sorting first responses to this location has taken some thought. Varying facts told during the tour and reading about ancient myths and legends have fuelled the initial images developed so far.

A well-defined network of tracks through the shrubs was observed. Apparently these were made by emus who always follow the same well worn 'walk about' paths. As with other Australian works, it is the dramatic colours and challenging tonal factors, that can transform a quite humble subject into interesting imagery. (see Book 22, Seeing Double)

Bold dimensional stitching was applied to capture the characteristics of the patterns inspired by the lunette's deeply fissured structures and can be seen as the experimental sample shown in the inside front cover. The third idea came from reading a book about Aboriginal myths. One of the legends told over the years says that *'the snake is female, creator of rainbows which she forms by blowing into the sky'*. This story appealed to a whimsical side of thought hence the design illustrated, which shows decorative rainbow devices placed rhythmically over the sinewy landscape formations.

rhythmic patterns in the sand
animal tracks, dots/dots/cracks /

More time is needed to peruse thoughts and memories or better still a return visit before embarking on further work. However, patterns taken out of context have proved to be an enjoyable starting point.

Below are listed some initial memories written on the journey home.

Space - amazing scale - wonderful patterns - dark and light ridges and shadows - fabulous colours - tracks in the sand - rivulets of sand, sinewy, rhythmic - fabulous colours in the sky before sunrise - turrets, ridges, crevices, ravines - turquoise shadows at sunset - scorpion holes - bright blue, green and pink parrots flying through the bush - blue/green shrubs - silver strands attached to the shrubs and floating in the air (supposedly kangaroo 'snot' marking territory as told by an Aboriginal Elder!) - ring around the sun - stars at night - rainbow snake story - Mallee gums - more ochre in colour than the Red Centre.

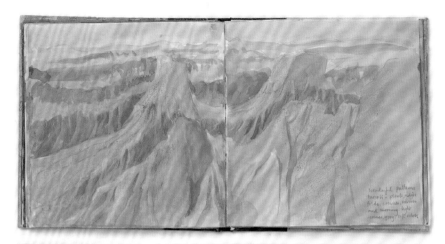

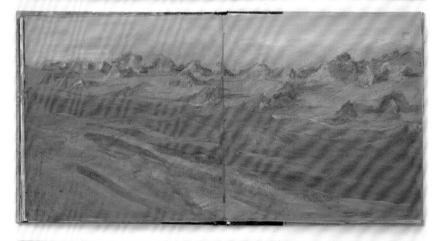

Having absorbed the overall feeling of colour and atmosphere, many of the pages were given a background of a colour wash before all the sketches were started in situ. During sketching, extensive colour notes were made. They were painted in more detail back at base using the notes along with memories to highlight and capture the essence of the place.

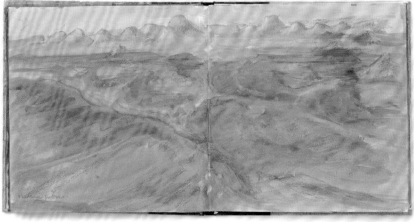

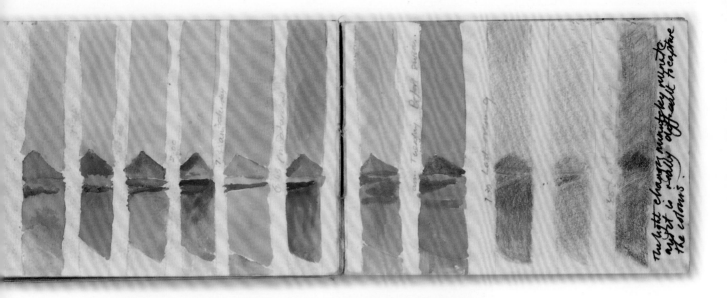

Themes: Spots and Stripes

Travel is said to broaden the mind and the sights, sounds, tastes and smells of a new place can overwhelm. Focussed looking helps to make sense of a new location or see a familiar view with fresh eyes.
Many people have found sketching and photography in a new location so much more satisfying when there is something specific to look for. We make no apology for repeating this useful advice when preparing for a journey and there are several different themes but those listed below might give you some ideas for notebooks of your own.

- Looking through
- Underfoot
- Aspects of decay
- Gateways and barriers
- Grids
- Textured surfaces
- Gaps and holes
- Reflections
- Edges
- Patterns and Rhythms
- Walls
- Tessellation
- Spots and stripes
- A colour

Initially, the challenge of spots and stripes may sound limiting but it soon becomes evident that it relates to multiple aspects of the world around us. Themes are not designed to restrict but to encourage lateral thinking.
Spots need not be rigid polka dots, they could be fluid spots of colour in a garden, pebbles on a beach or raindrops in a puddle. Stripes are all around us in barriers and fences as well as in stems, stalks and geological structures.

When considering spots it might be helpful to look at artists who have used them. The pointillists, Seurat, Signac and Pissaro could inspire a fresh way of looking. Damian Hurst and Bridget Riley both used spots and dots in significant series of works.

Pixilation in newspaper photographs could also be an interesting pathway and Roy Lichtenstein exploited them most successfully.

Of the numerous ways of making spots and stripes, printing with corks, ends of pencils and drinking straws might help.

Stripes can be drawn or painted in crisp or casual formations and they can also be printed using edges of cardboard, or plastic credit cards etc.

It can be most effective to create landscapes and other imagery using just spots or lines.

All the sketchbook pages shown here were worked in one location on holiday in Samos.

The book contained heavy watercolour paper and the materials used included Koh-i-Noor dyes, aquarelle pencils, graphite pencil, fine line pen and printing techniques.

The stripes (above) were slices of the same view seen through a balcony barrier at different times of day and varying light conditions.

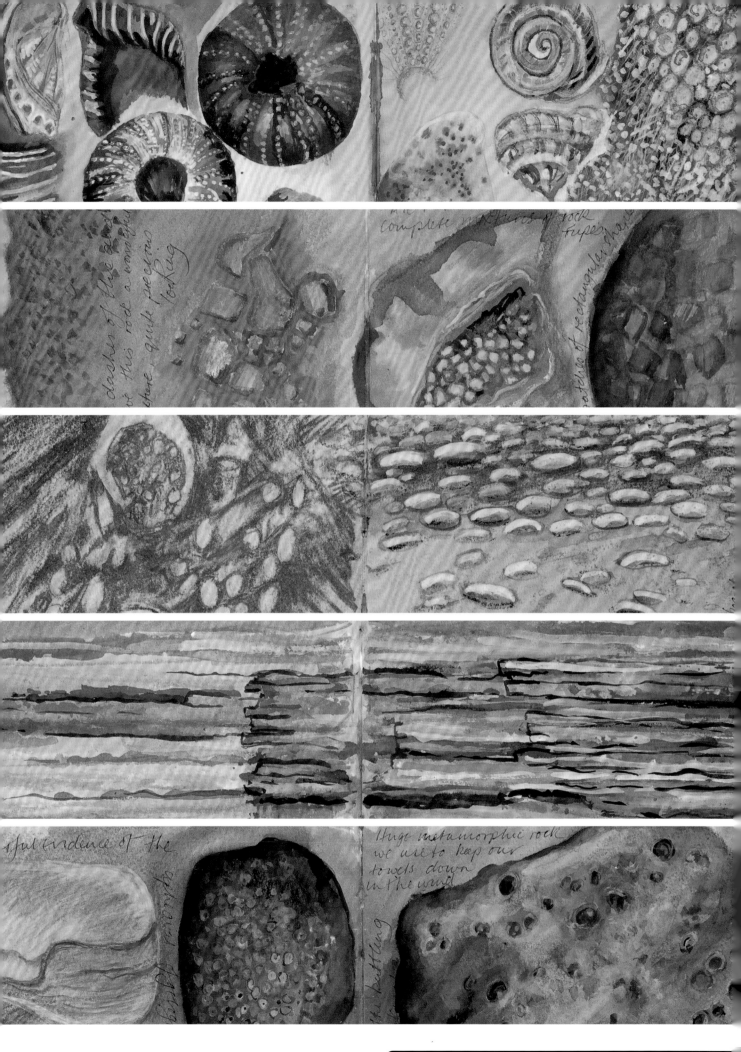

(2)

Walls

On walking around a familiar
neighbourhood find some
interesting walls to study.
A fabulous variety of walls can
be found throughout the world.

They could include the elegantly
patterned tiled walls of the
Alhambra Palace, in Granada,
Spain, old buildings in Corfu
where the eroded surfaces of
plaster expose the stone
structure beneath or a
traditional stone wall in rural
Britain where its crevices
harbour an array of mosses,
lichen and plant life.

A brick wall may be symmetrical
in its structure but the colourings
of the actual bricks are often
worth noticing related on their
age and from where they come.
Looking closely at just one brick
may well reveal an unexpected
colour scheme, which is worth
recording and may give a lift to
a jaded colour palette. Take care
to note the proportions of each
colour in order to retain the
initial attraction not allowing
the unexpected flashes of colour
to overwhelm and lose their
potency.

As well as being a means of
depicting a boundary, a wall can
support a range of plant life. The
mature, gnarled branch system
of the colourful blooms of a
Wisteria contrasts greatly with
the finer stem network of
Virginia Creeper.

Urban walls may have been used
as advertising hoardings and if
left in decline, the layers of
posters partially peeling away
plus the addition of graffiti can
capture a mood and be
fascinating to draw.

A sea wall constructed with
railway sleepers and ravaged over
time by extreme weather
conditions and seawater showed a
variety of remarkable colourings.
This included a range of putty,
grey and brown alongside tawny
hues of burnt sienna, orange,
ginger and ochre. The textures

were as equally exciting. Grooves,
ridges, crevices, flaky and organic
surfaces suggested a number of
stitch and fabric interpretations.
Patches, tucks and line stitches
worked in rich but subtle colours
could well influence the start of
some intriguing experimentation.

To record these observations,
determine the main characteristics
and first overall impression of the
surfaces being observed. Jot down
a list of describing words and/or
draw marks on some scrap paper
or on the edge of the sketchbook
page. It is worthwhile spending
time understanding the
underlying basic structure and not
being confused by details that can
be added later if appropriate.
Thinking simply helps with the
drawing process and the
collecting of information.
The following jottings illustrate
the initial starting thoughts
before embarking on the
sketches shown.

*Crete wall - crumbling, eroded,
rough edges
Sea wall - vertical lines, patches
of subtle colour
Old wall - feathery moss on top,
crumbly, lumpy, flaky,
undulating lichens,
tiny 'beaded' surface with
minute protruding short hairs.
Virginia Creeper - layers of
longish leaves hanging down in
vertical clumps
asymmetrical stem network -
red, plum, purple*

(1)

(4)

Layered painted and collaged papers were selected to make the sea wall sketch (1).

Pencil, aquarelle crayons and Koh-i-Noor paints were used to create the Corfu wall (2), Virginia Creeper (3) and old wall sketches (4).

It was easier to build up the old wall interpretation (above) with glued layers of a variety of white papers including tissue, cartridge and thin card attempting to create the flaky, undulating surface. Glass bead texture gel was employed to simulate another area.

After the piece was completely dry, colour was applied with a variety of paints (see right). This method of designing can be a useful link between a one dimensional sketch and working with textile media.

Gaps and Holes

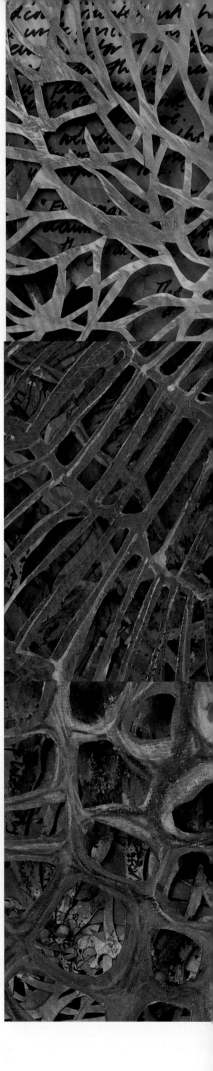

An annual holiday can be an opportunity to study and reflect on the immediate environment without the pressing distractions of home life. Before leaving, the travel design kit may need to be checked. It is almost impossible to replace some crucial materials in a remote location. Over a year tubes of gouache may look fine but have become hard and unusable.

Before a holiday in Lesbos our colleague Louise Baldwin had set the students a theme of networks and meshes and I determined beforehand to relate this to a personal interest in gaps and holes. This helped decide what type of sketchbook to take as it needed to have holes cut into the pages and a medium quality watercolour paper seemed best. A craft knife was also necessary and this needed to be packed in the hold luggage so as not to be confiscated at airport security. Drawing can take many forms and this was relatively new to me so I looked forward to responding to a fresh location with a new dynamic. I judged it unnecessary to take a cutting board and used magazines under the pages to protect the table. This resulted in masses of tiny cut paper shapes that blew about in the breeze and in future I would take the smallest board I could find.

The basic colour was once again 'Koh-i-Noor' with the addition of aquarelle crayons, fine pen and ink where necessary.

It was much easier to cut accurate shapes when the paper was completely dry so this needed to be factored in. When even slightly damp the shapes were difficult to cut and unsatisfactory. As I became used to the technique it really gathered momentum and it became a pleasure to seek out opportunities for layering up cut through imagery. The volcanic rocks were fissured with bubble like holes and the patterns under the water inspired a huge variety of networks and cut through patterns.

The completed sketchbook featured cutout formations and tied in with the lace like patterns of my current work

All the images on these pages relate to the gaps and holes notebook worked over a fortnight in Lesbos.

employing more refined developments such as silk screen techniques once back in a studio or workroom.

You can often doodle some ideas in a sketchbook while enjoying a cup of coffee or waiting for a train or plane. These first thoughts are often more spontaneous. Selecting a shape as an isolated pattern or as a repeating unit could be worked in a number of techniques.

If you have access to a computer, a decorative motif can be scanned and developed in many ways, changing the scale and colour to present a rich source of alternative results to consider. Some onlookers may find this approach rather static and too precise. However, making a repeating design can still be created without this aid and be most effective albeit not totally accurate with slightly quirky shapes.

Many of the patterns seen on Indian or African textiles are extremely attractive but none of the decorative components are the same although at first glance they appear so. Due to the balance and rhythm of all the elements and a rich or subtle colour palette, the overall effect is usually stunning.

On reaching home...

On arriving back at a base whether an apartment, hotel or at home, look carefully at the items you have collected. Many may have been picked up from the ground in the countryside or on a beach. It is always satisfying to mull over the varied assortment of leaves, flowers, stones, shells and the like. They will fuel your memories of a walk or a special place as well as offering possible design sources. Take care to note if there are any official notices requesting visitors not take away certain items due to their scarcity or historical significance. In this instance, sketch in situ, make lots of notes on colour, texture, etc. accompanied if possible by close-up photographs.

Organise your looking in order to isolate varying aspects. LOOK CLOSELY to identify colour schemes or to select unexpected shapes. These patterns taken out of context could be developed in a number of ways. Consider scanning, photocopying, drawing or painting the whole or part of each object. If appropriate some of the surfaces may be suitable to use for printing or for taking rubbings. Whatever method you choose, prolonged looking will reveal interesting surprises. A lino cut or card shapes assembled into a collaged design to make a printing block would suggest another approach. Printing with stencils and paper shapes could develop first ideas before

The sketchbook pages shown were all coloured before embarking on the drawings.

It is sometimes more comforting not to sketch on pristine white pages especially if you have an inkling of which sort of colour wash would be suitable for the place to be visited.

Assorted shells were collected from a beautiful sandy beach hence the pale coloured page. Back at base, studies were carried out using Koh-i-Noor and gouache paints.

Certain elements were selected out of context to form the repeating patterns shown and could be developed further to be worked in a variety of techniques.

Due to the darker pages, alternative methods of depicting the flattened magnolia seed head and squirrel-chewed pinecones were selected. White pencils and crayons were used to draw the basic shapes followed by further crayoning and the application of gouache paints as these have greater covering qualities.

The paler pages shown above seemed to be suitable for the subtle patterns and hues of fallen magnolia leaves. Silvery pewter, gold and grey colours predominated.

...and finally

After arriving home and packing everything away until the next holiday there is often a feeling of anticlimax. It is then good to look back at the holiday sketchbook and reflect on the sights and sensations of the experience. There might be times when the notebooks are complete and others when further working is needed.

'Koh-i-Noor' dyes work well as a vibrant portable colouring medium, but when dry lose some of the initial sparkle. The pages can be 'polished' with specialized waxes such as acrylic wax or wax varnish that add sheen and lustre (above). It is also possible to add shine by painting with watered down PVA glue.

Further detailing can also be worked with aquarelle pencils that are soft and effective on coloured grounds particularly with lighter colours for highlighting. Drawing inks add beautiful washes and lustre to emphasize areas as desired.

There is of course always the danger of overworking and it is best to leave well alone if there is a chance of spoiling an honest, raw if unpolished drawing that captured a moment.

If the imagery has been particularly inspiring then there are numerous ways in which to develop it further and in previous books we have detailed many such methods but where there is a new material that works well we like to explore it.

'PZkut' is a soft carving material that can be used in place of lino for prints. It cuts easily but care needs to be taken to avoid cutting hands with the carving tools. The patterns featured here were taken from a visit to Chinatown in Vancouver. The sketchbook drawing shows a detail from a lion carving and the heart shape was cut from the 'PZkut' and printed onto various coloured and prepared surfaces. These were combined with a second cut block based on a Chinese flower motif to produce more complex layered prints using acrylic paints and inks. Making many such prints in various colour ways will result in exciting and unexpected images that may also transfer to fabric and thread.

One print worked on rag paper was further developed with applied velvet shapes, hand and machine stitching (see right).

In this way with a combination of instant drawings, considered studies and design developments our visits to locations from near and far will refresh our ideas and inspire new work for years to come.

Double Trouble

Acknowledgments

Many thanks go to our husbands Philip Littlejohn and Steve Udall without whom Double Trouble could not function.
Our thanks also go to Jason Horsburgh for his care in designing our booklets and to Michael Wicks for his excellent photography.

The products and suppliers used in our books are listed at www.doubletrouble-ent.com